Background

EMBOSSING
WITH FRAMES

Anja van Laar

FORTE PUBLISHERS

Contents

ISBN 90 5877 454 6

This is a publication from
Forte Publishers BV
P.O. Box 1394
3500 BJ Utrecht
The Netherlands

For more information about the creative
books available from Forte Uitgevers:
www.forteuitgevers.nl

Final editing: Gina Kors-Lambers,
Steenwijk, the Netherlands
Photography and digital image editing:
Fotografie Gerhard Witteveen,
Apeldoorn, the Netherlands
Cover and inner design:
BADE creatieve communicatie, Baarn,
the Netherlands
Translation: Michael Ford, TextCase,
Hilversum, the Netherlands

Preface

Dear fellow crafters,

It is wonderful to receive so many positive reactions. I am always surprised that my efforts on the kitchen table have made so many people enthusiastic about card making. I have designed four new background embossing stencils and this time they have a frame in the middle. There are so many things you can do with them. In this book, I have not only used the new stencils, but also a number of the old stencils. I hope this book will show you some of the many different things you can do with them.

I wish you lots of fun!
Anja

Many thanks to Marianne for her enthusiasm and all the materials and everybody at home for their support, because sometimes I could no longer see the table under all the clutter.

Techniques

Embossing

Place the stencil on the good side of the card. Turn the stencil and the card over, place them on a light box and copy the illuminated shapes using the embossing stylus. If you wish, use Pergasoft (Pergamano) to make the embossing easier. If you are going to emboss a large area, then lightly rub a candle over the paper.

To prevent lines and scratches when embossing vellum, carefully start with a circular movement and then increase the pressure until the pattern becomes nice and white. For a larger pattern, start with a large embossing stylus and then go along the edges with a smaller stylus.

3D cutting and sticking

Cut the entire picture out for the first layer. For the next layer, decide what is in the background and do not cut that out. Cut out as many layers as you want in this way. If you do not use many layers, cut the incisions far into the paper and cut the front parts out completely. You can add as much or as little glue as you wish under the pictures, depending on the depth that you wish to create. If you put the glue in a syringe, you will have more control over the quantity of glue that you apply.

You can shape the pictures to help bring the 3D picture to life. You can do this using a shaping pen and a mat or you can simply use your fingers. For example, for a flower, shape the petals as much as possible as they are in real life. Experiment with 3D glue. For example, put more glue under the leaves to raise them slightly and put less glue in the middle of the flower so that you can push it down more. If you have separate petals which must be placed partially under another petal, then you must stick those down first. Push the petals down slightly where the other petal will be stuck on top.

Therefore, when making 3D pictures, make sure you do not simply stick all the parts down on top of each other.

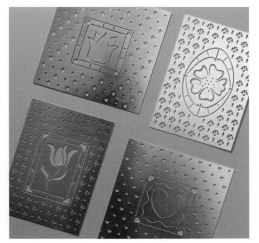

1. The new embossing stencils.

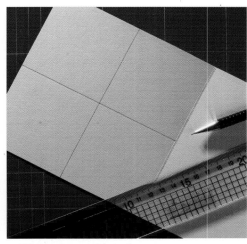

2. Divide the card into four.

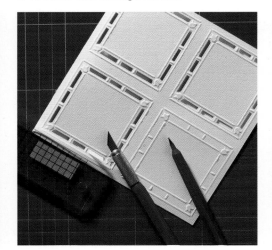

3. Emboss and cut the card.

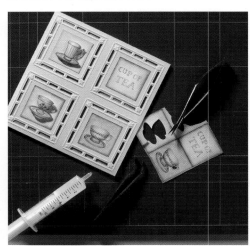

4. Decorate the card.

Materials

- Card:
  Canson Mi-Teintes (C)
  and Papicolor (P)
- Parchment/vellum
- Cutting sheets
- Embossing stencils
- Light box
- Embossing stylus
- Cutting mat
- Knife
- 3D scissors
- 3D glue
- Ruler
- Hole punch
- Circle cutter
- Photo glue
- Power Pritt (grey)
- Metal pendant
- Scrapbook basics
- Mini eyelets
- Eyelet tool
- Eyelet hammer

- Adhesive stones
- Cord
- Silver thread
- Ribbon
- Glitter
- Beads

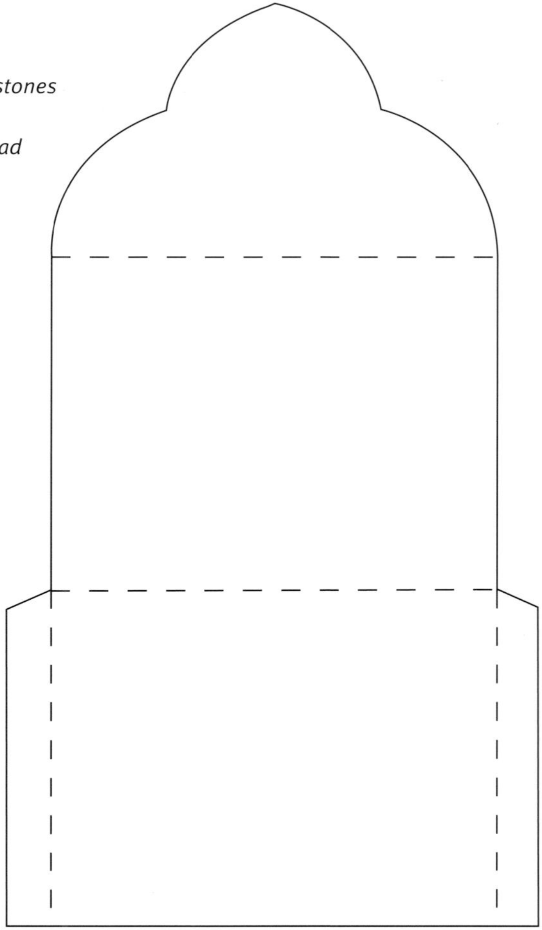

Diagram 1: envelope -
increase in size by 166%

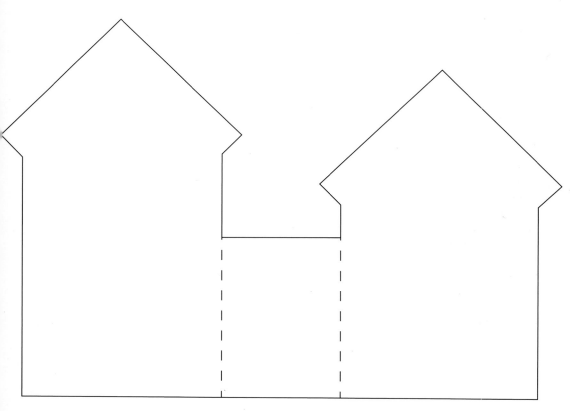

Diagram 2: increase in size by 154%

DIAGRAM 7

Congratulations

What you need
- ❏ *Card: pale yellow (P29),*
  wine red (P36) and olive green (P45)
- ❏ *Mattie de Bruine vellum:*
  Flowers MB 7013 and
  Leaves MB 7014
- ❏ *Mattie de Bruine cutting sheet: MB 0014*
- ❏ *Embossing stencils:*
  AE 1214, AE 1215 and AE 1217
- ❏ *Power Pritt*
- ❏ *Hole punch*
- ❏ *Gold cord*

1. Pink hydrangea

Make a wine red double card (13.5 x 13.5 cm) and stick pale yellow card (13 x 13 cm) on it.

Take a sheet of vellum (Flowers, 12.5 x 12.5 cm) and stick this on the card, but only apply glue in the middle. Use stencil no. 1215 to emboss the frame on pale yellow card. Cut out the pieces in the middle and then cut it out leaving a border. Stick it on wine red card and cut it out leaving a border. Stick everything on the card. Stick the picture on the card and make it 3D.

2. Blue hydrangea

Take a piece of pale yellow card (19 x 17.5 cm) and fold it 7 cm from the left-hand side. Use

stencil no. 1215 to emboss dots on it. Take a piece of olive green card (19 x 7.2 cm) and stick it behind the front flap. Stick vellum (Leaves) behind the green card and then pale yellow card behind the vellum. Use stencil no. 1215 to emboss the shape on pale yellow card. Cut out the pieces in the middle and then cut out the shape leaving a border. Stick it on olive green card and cut it out leaving a border. Use the hole punch to punch two holes in the card and one hole in the label. Take some gold cord and tie it in a pretty bow to attach the label to the card. Stick the pictures on the card and make them 3D.

1.

2.

3.

4.

5.

frame twice on pale yellow card and cut them out as shown in the photograph. Stick one frame on the card and the other on a sheet of vellum (leaves) before sticking it on the card. Use 3D glue to stick pictures on the card and make them 3D.

3. Pumpkin

Take a piece of pale yellow card (23 x 13.5 cm) and fold it 9.5 cm from the top. Use stencil no. 1214 to emboss squares on it. Take a piece of wine red card (13.5 x 9.7 cm) and stick it behind the front flap. Stick olive green card (13.5 x 13.5 cm) behind the wine red card. Stick the pictures on the card and make them 3D.

4. Triptych

Make a wine red triptych card according to diagram 2. Use stencil no. 1215 to emboss the

5. Gift envelope

Use vellum (Leaves) to make an envelope according to diagram 1. Make a wine red double card (9 x 7 cm) with the fold at the top. Use stencil no. 1217 to emboss the frame on pale yellow card. Cut out the pieces in the middle and then cut it out leaving a border. Stick the frame on the card and add a 3D picture. Add some stickers.

Will you marry me?

What you need
- ❏ Card: mango (P40) and gravel (125 g. and 175 g.) (P161 Brilliant)
- ❏ Perkaline parchment: jade 155
- ❏ Mattie de Bruine cutting sheet: MB 0025
- ❏ Embossing stencils:
  AE 1214, AE 1215, AE 1216 and AE 1217
- ❏ Power Pritt
- ❏ Metal pendants
- ❏ Hole punch
- ❏ Silver ribbon
- ❏ Gold cord

1. Label card
Take a piece of thin gravel card (29.7 x 18 cm) and fold it 8.8 cm from both sides. Use stencil no. 1217 to emboss the background and then stick mango card behind it. Use stencil no. 1217 to emboss the frame on mango card and cut out the middle pieces as shown in the photograph. Stick it on jade parchment and cut it out leaving a border. Use a needle to prick two holes in the label and thread a gold cord through them. Stick the ends of the cord to the back of the card. Use 3D glue to stick pictures on the card.

2. Say it with roses
Take a piece of thick gravel card (29.7 x 10.5 cm) and fold it 10.7 cm from the side. Use stencil no. 1214 to emboss the background. Stick mango card (10.9 cm) behind the front flap and then stick a piece of jade parchment (19 x 10.5 cm) behind the mango card. Take a strip of mango card (10.5 x 2.7 cm) and stick gravel card (10.5 x 2.5 cm) on it. Stick this on the card as shown in the photograph. Stick the picture on the card and make it 3D.

3. Good luck

Make a mango double card (14 x 14 cm) with the fold on the left-hand side. Take a piece of thin gravel card (13.5 x 13.5 cm), use stencil no. 1215 to emboss the background on it and stick it on the card. Use the hole punch to make two holes in the front flap. Thread silver ribbon through

the holes and tie it in a pretty bow. Hang the pendants on the ends of the ribbon. Stick the picture on the card and make it 3D.

4. Envelope

Use jade parchment to make an envelope according to diagram 1. Make a gravel double card (8.5 x 5.5 cm). Use stencil no. 1215 to emboss dots on it. Use stencil no. 1214 to emboss the heart twice on gravel card and cut them out leaving a border. Stick one on jade parchment and one on mango card and cut them out leaving a border. Stick them on the card as shown in the

photograph. Use 3D glue for the heart on the right-hand side. Add a 3D picture and a sticker.

5. Arum lily

Take a piece of thin gravel card (29.7 x 18 cm) and fold it 8.8 cm from both sides. Make the left-hand flap as shown in the photograph. First, use a pencil to mark the point of the flap and use it to cut the corners at an angle. Stick mango card behind it and cut it off leaving a 2 mm wide border. Use stencil no. 1216 to emboss the background on the other flap. Make a 2.5 cm long incision in the card as shown in the photograph. Take a piece of jade parchment (18 x 12 cm) and use Power Pritt to stick it on the middle section inside the card. Stick a picture on the card and make it 3D.

Are you ill?

What you need
- ❏ Card:
   high yellow (C400) and orange (C453)
- ❏ Pergamano vellum: green (100 g.) (1608)
- ❏ Picturel cutting sheets: 0548 and 0549
- ❏ Embossing stencils:
   AE 1215, AE 1216 and AE 1217
- ❏ Power Pritt
- ❏ Scrapbook basics: Roses and Corners
- ❏ Hole punch
- ❏ Gold cord

1. Get well soon

Take a piece of yellow card (29.7 x 10.5 cm) and fold it double. Use stencil no. 1216 to emboss the oval as shown in the photograph, with both halves 1 cm from the edge of the card. Cut the middle pieces out. Use stencil no. 1216 to emboss the background. Stick orange card behind the front flap. Use stencil no. 1216 to emboss the flower on green vellum and cut it out leaving a border. Stick it on yellow card and cut it out leaving a border. Use the hole punch to make a hole in the label. Wind gold cord around the front flap of the card and tie a pretty bow to attach the label to the card. Stick a picture on the card and make it 3D. Add some stickers.

2. Would you like some grapes?

Take a piece of yellow card (19.5 x 13.5 cm) and fold it 6 cm from the left-hand side. Stick orange card (13.5 x 6.2 cm) behind the front flap. Take a sheet of green vellum (10.5 x 7 cm) and fold it 1 cm from the left-hand side. Use stencil no. 1217 to emboss the background on the 6 cm wide strip. Use Power Pritt to stick the vellum to the back of the card. Use stencil

no. 1215 to emboss the flower on yellow card and cut it out leaving a border. Stick it on orange card and cut it out leaving a border. Use the hole punch to make two holes in the card and one hole in the label. Use gold cord to attach the label to the card. Use 3D glue to

stick a picture on the card and make it 3D.
Add some stickers.

3. Oranges

Make an orange double card (13.5 x 13.5 cm)
and stick yellow card (12.5 x 12.5 cm) on it.
Take a sheet of green vellum (12 x 12 cm) and
use stencil no. 1216 to emboss the background
on it. Use Power Pritt to stick it on the card.
Only apply the Power Pritt to the middle and the
corners so that it cannot be seen. Stick a picture
on the card and make it 3D. Stick some corner
stickers on the card.

4. Gift envelope

Use green vellum to make an envelope according
to diagram 1. Stick roses on the envelope. Take a
piece of yellow card (16 x 7 cm) and fold it 6.5 cm
and 9.5 cm from the side. Use stencil no. 1216 to
emboss half an oval on the left and right-hand
flaps. Cut the middle pieces out and then cut the
half ovals out leaving a border. Cut a 1 cm wide
strip from the top and bottom of the middle part
of the card. Stick the pictures on the card and
make them 3D. Add some stickers.

5. Fruit basket

Take a piece of yellow card (29.7 x 10.5 cm) and

fold it 11.2 cm from the left-hand side. Use
stencil no. 1216 to emboss the flowers. Stick
orange card (11.4 x 10.5 cm) behind the front
flap. Stick green vellum (18.5 x 10.5 cm) behind
the orange card and then stick yellow card
(18.5 x 10.5 cm) behind the green vellum.
Use 3D glue to stick the picture on the card
and make it 3D. Stick some corner stickers on
the card.

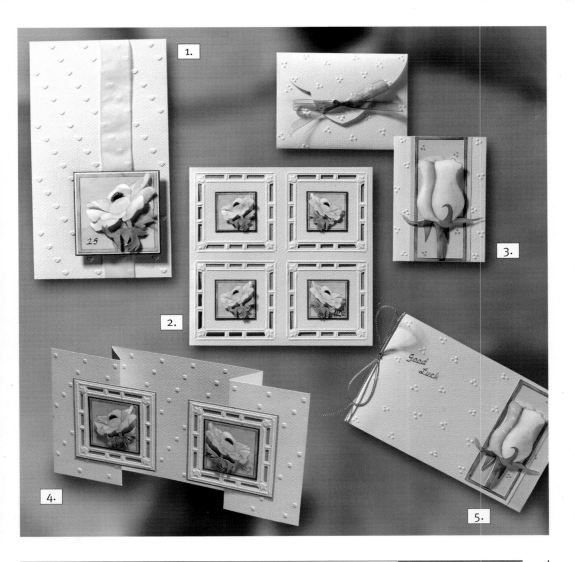

1.

2.

3.

4.

5.

Anniversary

What you need
- ❏ *Card: ivory (C111), dark green (C448)*
  and almond green (C480)
- ❏ *Marjoleine cutting sheets:*
  Flowers and Pattern 2
- ❏ *Embossing stencils:*
  AE 1214, AE 1215 and AE 1217
- ❏ *Gold cord*
- ❏ *Organza ribbon:*
  green (0.5 cm wide) and cream (2.5 cm wide)
- ❏ *Mini eyelets (gold)*

1. 25th anniversary

Make an ivory double card (19 x 10.5 cm).
Use stencil no. 1214 to emboss hearts on it.
Take cream Organza ribbon and tie it around
the card. Stick the ends of the ribbon on the
card where the picture will be stuck on the
card. Cut the picture out, stick it on ivory
card and cut it out
leaving a border. Stick
it on dark green card
and cut it out leaving a
border. Use 3D glue to
stick it on the card and
make the picture 3D.
Add a sticker.

2. Collage card

Make an ivory double card (14 x 14 cm) and use
a pencil to divide the back of the front flap into
four sections. Use stencil no. 1215 to emboss

the frames using the pencil lines as a guide.
Cut the middle pieces out. Take a piece of
almond green card (14 x 14 cm) and stick it
inside the card next to the fold using only a
small strip of glue. Stick the pictures on dark
green card and cut them out leaving a border.
Stick everything on the card and make the
pictures 3D. Add a sticker.

3. Gift envelope

Use ivory card to make an envelope according to diagram 1. Before sticking it together, use stencil no. 1217 to emboss dots on it as shown in the photograph. Next, punch four eyelets in the envelope: two in the flap and two under the flap. Take green Organza ribbon and thread it through the bottom eyelets. Stick down the sides of the envelope. Do not tie a bow in the Organza ribbon until the card has been put in the envelope. Make an ivory double card (9.7 x 7 cm) and stick pattern paper (9.7 x 4.6 cm) on it. Cut the picture out as shown in the photograph and stick it on the card. Use stencil no. 1217 to emboss some dots. Make the picture 3D.

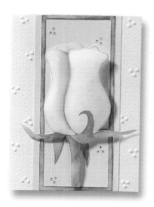

4. Forty years together

Take a piece of ivory card (29.6 x 10.5 cm) and fold it four times: 5.8 cm and 8.8 cm from the left-hand side and 5.8 cm and 8.8 cm from the right-hand side. Use stencil no. 1214 to emboss the squares. Use stencil no. 1215 to emboss the frame twice on ivory card. Cut the middle pieces out and then cut the frames out leaving a border. Stick them on almond green card and cut them out leaving a border. Stick the frames on the card as shown in the photograph. Stick the pictures on dark green card and cut them out leaving a border. Make the pictures 3D and add a sticker.

5. Good luck

Take a piece of ivory card (29.7 x 9.7 cm) and fold it 14.2 cm from the left-hand side. Stick the picture on the front flap. Cut away the card between the edge of the picture and the rose. Use stencil no. 1217 to emboss the dots on the card in groups of three as shown in the photograph. Stick pattern paper (15.5 x 9.7 cm) on the rear flap. Tie gold cord around the card and tie it in a pretty bow. Add a 3D picture and some stickers.

For the kids

What you need
- ❏ Card:
    high yellow (C400) and bright red (C506)
- ❏ Picturel vellum 1547
- ❏ Picturel cutting sheets:
    0545, 0547 and 0549
- ❏ Embossing stencils:
    AE 1214, AE 1215 and AE 1217
- ❏ Funny Fibres: yellow
- ❏ Scrapbook basics: Pets
- ❏ Adhesive stones: red
- ❏ Eyelets: yellow
- ❏ Circle cutter
- ❏ Power Pritt

1. Round card

Make a circle (Ø 12 cm) from red card. Use stencil no. 1215 to emboss dots on it. Stick it on a yellow circle (Ø 12.5 cm). Use stencil no. 1214 to emboss the frame on yellow card. Cut out the pieces in the middle and then cut the frame out leaving a border. Stick the frame on the card and add two eyelets. Thread yellow cord through the eyelets and secure the cord by tying a knot in the ends. Stick a picture on the card and make it 3D. Stick adhesive stones on the card.

2. Pick a rose

Take a piece of red card (29.7 x 10.5 cm) and fold it 10.2 cm from the right-hand side. Use stencil no. 1215 to emboss dots as shown in photograph. Take a piece of yellow card (17 x 10.5 cm), fold it 1 cm from the left-hand side and stick it on the red card. Cut the yellow flap into a point. Use a pencil to mark points at the top and the bottom 9.5 cm from the right-hand side. Use stencil no. 1215 to emboss the flowers. Use stencil no. 1215 to emboss the figure on yellow card and cut it out leaving a border. Stick it on red card and cut it out leaving a border. Use 3D glue to stick it on the card, making sure you can slide the yellow flap underneath. Stick a picture on the card and make it 3D. Add a sticker.

3. Welcome to the ball

Take a piece of yellow card (21 x 19.5 cm) and fold it 4.5 cm from the left-hand side. Use stencil no. 1214 to emboss the squares. Stick red card (21 x 4.7 cm) behind the front flap and

then stick vellum and yellow card (21 x 15 cm) behind it. Use stencil no. 1214 to emboss a heart on red and on yellow card and cut them out leaving a border. Use the hole punch to punch two holes in the card and one hole in the hearts. Use yellow cord to attach the hearts and the bone on the card. Stick a picture on the card and make it 3D. Add a sticker.

4. The bear doctor

Take a piece of yellow card (29.7 x 10.5 cm) and fold it six times: 11 cm, 12.6 cm, 14.2 cm, 25.3 cm, 26.9 cm and 28.5 cm from the left-hand side. There will now be two large areas which are 11.1 cm wide which are the front and back of the card. The smallest strip is the strip for sticking the card together. The other bits are the sides. Make sure you fold the sides into a zigzag shape. Use stencil no. 1217 to emboss the frame on the front of the card and cut out the middle pieces. Use stencil no. 1214 to emboss hearts. Stick red card

(11.1 x 10.5 cm) on the rear flap inside the card. Stick the pictures on the card and make them 3D. Stick some adhesive stones on the card.

5. What a lot of bears

Take a piece of yellow card (29.7 x 5 cm) and fold it 9.9 cm and 19.8 cm from the side. Use stencil no. 1217 to emboss the triangles. Use stencil no. 1214 to emboss the frame three times on yellow card. Cut the middle pieces out and then cut the frames out leaving a border. Stick the frames on red card and cut them out leaving a border. Stick them on the card as shown in the photograph. Use 3D glue to stick the pictures on the card.

It's autumn!

What you need
- Card:
  cream (P27) and light green (P47)
- Pergamano parchment: Fantasy purple 1656
- Diny cutting sheets: Rosehip and Autumn
- Embossing stencils:
  AE 1214, AE 1215, AE 1216 and AE 1217
- Silver pendants
- Organza ribbon: brown (3 mm wide)
- Silver chord
- Pearl beads: assorted
- Eyelets: silver
- Glitter: Stickles Copper and Stickles Icicle
- Power Pritt

1. For no reason
Use purple parchment to make an envelope
according to diagram 1 and use stencil no. 1216
to emboss the flowers on it as shown in the
photograph. Punch two eyelets in the flap.
Use the hole punch to make two holes under
the flap. Thread silver cord through the holes.
Stick down the sides of the envelope. Tie a bow
in the silver cord and attach the pendants after
the card has been placed in the envelope. Make
a cream double card (7 x 7 cm), use stencil
no. 1214 to emboss the frame on it and cut the

middle pieces out. Take a sheet of purple
parchment (7 x 7 cm) and stick it inside the
card by putting glue on only a small strip of
the parchment. Use 3D glue to stick a picture
on the card. Add a sticker and apply some
copper glitter to the picture.

2. Rosehip
Make a cream double card (14.8 x 10.5 cm).
Stick the picture on purple parchment, cut it out
leaving a border and stick it on the card. Use
stencil no. 1217 to emboss the triangles. Make
the pictures 3D and add some copper glitter.

3. What a picture!

Make a light green double card (13.5 x 13.5 cm). Use stencil no. 1215 to emboss the frame on the inside of the front flap, making sure the frame is exactly in the middle. Cut the middle pieces out. Next, cut around the right-hand half of the square. Fold the card's front flap double as shown in the photograph (score the fold line first). Take a sheet of purple parchment (13.5 x 13.5 cm) and use stencil no. 1215 to emboss the flowers on it. Stick it on the card by putting glue on only a small strip of the parchment. Use stencil no. 1215 to emboss the figure on cream card and cut it out leaving a border. Stick it on purple parchment and cut it out leaving a border. Use the hole punch to punch a hole in the card and the label. Fold a piece of silver cord double and attach it to the card as shown in the photograph. Attach the label and a pendant to the ends. Stick the pictures on the card and make them 3D. Add some (Icicle) glitter.

4. Autumn

Take a piece of light green card (29.5 x 10.5 cm) and fold it 10.5 cm from the left-hand side. Use stencil no. 1215 to emboss dots on it. Take a sheet of purple parchment (10 x 10 cm) and use

Power Pritt to stick it on the card. Only apply glue to the middle so that it cannot be seen. Stick a picture on the card and make it 3D. Add some stickers. Use a needle to prick two holes in the side of the card and thread silver cord through them. Thread the pearl beads and the pendants on the cord and tie knots in the ends. Add some copper glitter to the pictures.

5. Triptych

Make a cream triptych card according to diagram 3. Use stencil no. 1217 to emboss the background on the left-hand side. Also emboss the background on the right-hand side as shown in the photograph. Use stencil no. 1217 to emboss the frame on light green card. Cut out the pieces in the middle and then cut the frame out leaving a border. Stick the frame on purple parchment and cut it out leaving a border. Stick this on the right-hand side of the card. Use stencil no. 1217 to emboss the flower on cream card and cut it out leaving a border. Use 3D glue to stick it on the card. Use Organza ribbon to tie an attractive bow around it and attach pendants to the ends of the ribbon. Stick a picture on the left-hand side of the card and make it 3D. Add some copper glitter.

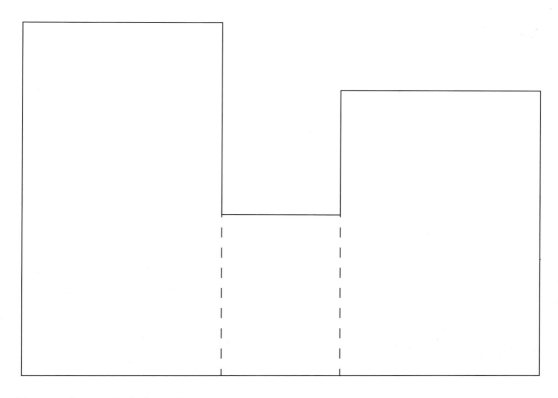

Diagram 3: increase in size by 154%

Winter

What you need

- Card:
  wine red (P36), light green (P47)
  and gravel (175 g.) (P161 Brilliant)
- Mattie de Bruine vellum:
  MB 7017 and MB 7021
- Mattie de Bruine cutting sheet: MB 0023
- Embossing stencils: AE 1204, AE 1206,
  AE 1212, AE 1213, AE 1215, AE 1216 and AE 1217
- Gold cord
- Ribbon
- Hole punch
- Power Pritt

1. For Grandma

Make a gravel double card (13.5 x 13.5 cm).
Use stencil no. 1206 to emboss the tulip at the
top of the front flap in the middle. Use stencil
no. 1212 to emboss the straight lines and stencil
no. 1204 to emboss the curved lines as shown
in the photograph. Cut it out as shown in the

picture. Place the ruler along the straight lines
and cut the rear of the card away along the
ruler. Use stencil no. 1215 to emboss the
flowers. Add a 3D picture and some stickers.

2. A bunch of tulips for you

Make a gravel double card (21 x 10.5 cm). Use
stencil no. 1212 to emboss the straight lines in
the top right-hand corner (upright line = 9 cm).
Use stencil no. 1204 to emboss the curved lines
as shown in the photograph. Cut out the card
between the lines leaving a border. Use stencil
no. 1217 to emboss the background. Cut vellum
to the correct size and use Power Pritt to stick it
behind the areas which have been cut open.
Take a piece of light green card (21 x 10.5 cm)
and stick it behind the front flap next to the fold
using only a small strip of glue. Use stencil
no. 1215 to emboss the shape on gravel card
and cut it out leaving a border. Stick a picture
on the card and make it 3D, making sure to
leave some space for the cord. Tie gold cord
around a stem of the bunch of tulips and add
the label. Add some stickers.

3. Thank you!

Make a gravel double card (19 x 12.5 cm). Use stencil no. 1216 to emboss the frame in the middle. Make a template (14.5 x 8 cm) from a scrap piece of card, place it in the middle of the card and use a pencil to mark the corners. Note: it is difficult to rub pencil marks off of this type of card. Place the ruler from corner to corner, mark the middle and draw 1 cm wide strips going to the embossed frame. Cut the card away along the pencil lines as shown in the photograph. Use stencil no. 1217 to emboss the dots in groups of three over the card. Cut vellum to the correct size and use Power Pritt to stick it behind the front of the card. Cut light green card to the correct size and stick it on the rear flap next to the fold using only a small strip of glue. Stick a picture on the card and make it 3D.

4. Hellebore

Make a gravel double card (13.5 x 13.5 cm). Cut the front flap diagonally through the middle as shown in the photograph. Use stencil no. 1212 to emboss the lines. Cut vellum to the correct size and use Power Pritt to stick it behind the front flap. Stick light green card (13.5 x 13.5 cm) behind it next to the fold using only a small strip of glue. Use stencil no. 1215 to emboss the frame on gravel card. Cut out the pieces in the middle leaving a border and then cut the frame out leaving a border. Stick the frame on wine red card, cut it out leaving a border and stick it on the card. Stick a picture on the card and make it 3D.

5. Hello

Take a piece of gravel card (24 x 10.5 cm) and fold it 4 cm from the left-hand side. Use stencil no. 1212 to emboss the flowers on the flap. Cut two gravel rectangles (10.5 x 4 cm) and emboss the flowers on them. Cut two strips of vellum, making sure that the flowers are in the middle. Use Power Pritt to stick one strip of vellum to the front flap, followed by a strip of gravel card, the other strip of vellum and, finally, another strip of gravel card. The front of the card will now be divided into five pieces which are each 4 cm wide. Take a piece of light green card (20 x 10.5 cm) and stick it behind the front flap next to the fold using only a small strip of glue. Use stencil no. 1213 to emboss the hat on gravel card and cut it out leaving a border. Stick it on wine red card and cut it out leaving a border. Use the hole punch to make a hole in the label. Tie a piece of ribbon around the card and attach the label. Use 3D glue to stick the picture on the card. Add a sticker.

Christmas

What you need

- *Card:*
  off-white (C110) and dark blue (C500)
- *Pergamano vellum: red 1639 (90 g.)*
- *Diny cutting sheets: 432 and 435*
- *Embossing stencils:*
  AE 1207, AE 1208, AE 1214,
  AE 1215, AE 1216 and AE 1217
- *Power Pritt*
- *Gold cord*
- *Mini eyelets: red*
- *Organza ribbon: red (3 mm wide)*
- *Glitter Writers Sparkles*

1. Christmas

Make a white double card (14 x 14 cm) and use a pencil to divide the back of the front flap into four sections. Use stencil no. 1215 to emboss the squares using the pencil lines as a guide.

Emboss the flowers in the bottom left-hand corner and the top right-hand corner. Cut out the middle pieces of the squares. Stick red vellum (14 x 14 cm) behind the front flap next to the fold using only a small strip of glue. Stick pictures on the card and make one of them 3D. Add some glitter.

2. Long branch

Take a piece of red vellum (29.7 x 10.5 cm). Fold it double and keep the fold at the top. Use stencil no. 1208 to emboss stars on it. Cut a white strip (29.7 x 8 cm), fold it double and keep the fold at the top. Use stencil no. 1207 to emboss two straight lines on the front flap. Move the stencil to make the lines longer and continue embossing the lines. Use the same stencil to emboss the two curved lines. Use stencil no. 1207 to emboss the short lines between the straight lines and the curved lines as shown in the photograph. Cut the middle pieces out and cut around the outer lines leaving a border. Place the ruler along the embossed straight lines and cut the back to the same width. Stick it on the front of the card. Take a piece of blue card (14.3 x 7.5 cm) and stick it on the card. Add a 3D picture and some glitter.

3. Label card

Make a white double card (14 x 14 cm) and stick a picture on it. Use stencil no. 1214 to emboss the squares around it. Cut the four points out of the picture as shown in the photograph and stick red vellum (7 x 7 cm) behind it. Use stencil no. 1216 to emboss the shape on white card and cut it out leaving a border. Stick it on blue card and cut it out leaving a border. Punch two eyelets in the card and one eyelet in the label. Thread gold cord through the eyelets and tie a pretty bow to attach the label to the card. Make the pictures 3D and add some glitter.

4. Where is my beak?

Make a red vellum double card (18.5 x 10.5 cm) and a white double card (15 x 10.5 cm). Have the fold of both cards on the left-hand side. Use stencil no. 1207 to emboss the curved lines as shown in the photograph, keeping approximately 1.5 cm between the two lines at the top. Use stencil no. 1207 to emboss the short lines. Cut the middle pieces out and then cut along the outer lines leaving a border. Use stencil no. 1215 to emboss dots on it. Stick everything on the red card next to the fold using only a small strip of glue. Stick a picture on the card and make it 3D. Add some glitter.

5. Merry Christmas and a Happy New Year

Take a piece of red vellum (29.6 x 9.5 cm) and fold it three times to make four parts which are 7.4 cm wide. The first fold is 7.4 cm from the side, the second 14.8 cm and the third 22.2 cm. Use stencil no. 1217 to emboss the frame four times on white card. Cut the middle pieces out of two frames. Cut out all the frames leaving a border and stick them on the card as shown on the photograph. Use stencil no. 1217 to emboss the flower on white card and cut it out leaving a border. Use red ribbon to tie a pretty bow and use 3D glue to stick it on the card. Stick the pictures on the card and make them 3D. Add some stickers and some glitter.

Many thanks to
Avec BV in Waalwijk, the Netherlands •
Kars en Co BV in Ochten, the Netherlands
• Papicolor International BV in Utrecht,
the Netherlands • Pergamano International
in Uithoorn, the Netherlands for supplying
the materials

Shopkeepers can order the materials from the companies listed above.

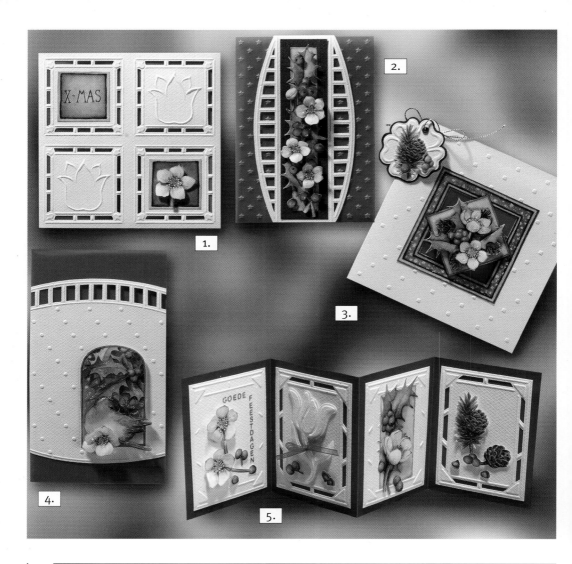